# Central Glasgow in the 70s

## Peter Mortimer & Duncan McCallum

In the foreground is Glasgow Cross Station built in 1896 by the Glasgow Central Railway Co. shown here as it was in April 1973. Following the rationalisation of the rail network, it closed in 1964 and was later demolished. The background is dominated by the offices of the City Council. A plaque on the wall, close to the corner with Albion Street marks the location where James Watt had a workshop. An instrument maker at the University of Glasgow, whilst taking a stroll on Glasgow Green had the idea of using a separate condenser for the steam engine, making it much more efficient, and made the Industrial Revolution possible.

Stenlake Publishing Ltd

© 2015 Peter Mortimer & Duncan McCallum
First Published in the United Kingdom, 2015
Stenlake Publishing Limited
54-58 Mill Square, Catrine, KA5 6RD
www.stenlake.co.uk

Printed by P2D Books, 1 Newlands Rd, Westoning, Bedford, MK45 5LD

ISBN 9781840337235

# Acknowledgements

Many thanks to everyone who encouraged us to produce this book, also Alistair Dinsmor, John Gorevan, and Norrie McNamee.

# Further Reading

*The Glasgow Encyclopedia*, Joe Fisher
*Glasgow Street Names*, Carol Foreman
*Glasgow Pubs and Publicans*, John Gorevan
*Architecture of Glasgow,* Andor Gomme & David Walker
*Public Sculpture*, Ray McKenzie
*Origin of Glasgow Street Names*, Hugh Mackintosh
*Glasghu Facies*, John McUre
*A Guide to Glasgow Addresses*, Susan Miller
*Pioneering the Health of the City*, Ronnie Scott
*Tinderbox Heroes*, Aland Forbes & James Smith
*The Glasgow Almanac*, Stephen Terry

*The Buildings of Glasgow*, Williamson, Riches & Higgs
*Historical Directory to Glasgow Presbytery*

**WEBPAGES**
www.secretscotland.uk
www.glasgowtransport.co.uk
www.scottisharchitects.org.uk
www.oldglasgowpubs.co.uk
www.fireheritagetrail.org
www.horseshoebar.co.uk
www.holroydgallery.co.uk

Nicholas Street looking towards the Old College Bar.

# Introduction

When Duncan McCallum walked the streets of Glasgow in the early 1970s photographing everyday scenes, he made an invaluable archive. The city centre has been through a period of considerable change in recent years, with many old buildings being lost to the bulldozer, and yet many old favourites still survive. This journey through the city centre will see examples of both, stretching from Glasgow Cross into the Bridgegate, the historic High Street as well as the commercial district in the heart of the city centre.

This view of the south-west corner of Glasgow Cross shows two contrasting designs of tenements. Nos. 8 to 30 Saltmarket are quite plain by comparison to the adjacent No. 3 Trongate. The Trongate tenement extends along to Chisholm Street and was built between 1891 and 1900 to a design by A.B. McDonald, the architect for Glasgow Corporation. The style is distinctly French Renaissance, with conical towers, pedimented dormers and a balustrade. At the time of their construction they were very desirable. The houses were large (three or four apartments) with bathrooms, at a time when many tenements had a shared toilet on the common landing. Although photographed in November 1973 this view remains largely unaltered today.

The old police headquarters and District Court building began life as a family home, built in 1896 to a design by A. B. McDonald, for use by widowed men and their children. The men would be able to go to work whilst their children were looked after and sent to school. In 1931 the building became the Administrative Headquarters for the City of Glasgow Police, and by the late 1970s was in use as the District Court. Next door, and divided by London Lane, is the Tontine Hotel, a former warehouse opened in 1926 to accommodate 303 persons, living in dormitories holding around 35 cubicles. It was one of numerous hotels in the city providing a place for people of very modest means to live and provided a restaurant serving meals at value prices. In June 1974 an elderly resident died in a fire and a few weeks later it closed for good, as its fire safety arrangements were not adequate.

St. Andrew's Street seen here in March 1973, was laid out in the late 18th century on the line of a thoroughfare known as Baxter's Wynd. Nos. 12 to 18 and 28 to 32 display attractive frontages, with crow stepped pediments and oriel windows from the first floor upwards, whilst wedged between them is the plain fronted tenement at Nos. 20 to 24, which looks rather out of place, and raises the question of why it wasn't a continuation of its neighbours to complete the terrace.

To the left on this view of St. Andrew's Square, stands the three storey high City Orphan Home built in 1876 to a design by Robert Bryden with a lift housing added later. It was built for William Quarrier, who took a keen interest in supporting disadvantaged children. Quarrier, born in Greenock in 1829, achieved success in business. He opened his first home for children in 1871 at Cowcaddens. The Quarriers organisation later relocated to their purpose-built village near Bridge of Weir where children in their care were looked after, received an education, and prepared for life in the adult world. The City Orphan Home has been converted into flats (minus the unsightly lift housing). On the right is St. Andrew's Parish Church, which was completed in 1756.

From left to right we have the edge of the Tannery Building in St. Andrew's Square, the side elevation of the Tent Hall, and the Central Police Buildings in Turnbull Street. The Tannery Building was the leather works of John Inglis & Co., and dates from 1877. Like many commercial buildings in the area, it has been converted into a housing development. The building further down with the pointed gable is the Tent Hall at Steel Street, and closer to the camera rising up the incline is the impressive Central Police Buildings, opened in 1908 which housed a police station and court room, and in more recent times became the City of Glasgow Police Museum. It is currently in a state of disrepair.

The Ship Bank was established at the corner of Saltmarket and Bridgegate in 1750 and was among the most successful of the 18th century Glasgow banks. Glasgow's rapid expansion during this period made a ready market for banks to handle money and give loans. Other banks such as The Glasgow Arms Bank, The Merchant Bank and Thomson's Bank didn't fare as well as The Ship Bank, and all of them failed in 1793. The Ship Bank eventually became part of the Bank of Scotland, and its ship emblem can still be seen on the back of some Bank of Scotland notes. The tenement and public house date from 1849, and were remodelled in 1904.

Looking east along Bridgegate at St. Margaret's Place in March 1973, we see the gentle curve from Saltmarket, which in former times led to the foot of Stockwell Street, at the bridge over the River Clyde, hence the name Bridgegate, or 'Briggit'. It is one of the oldest streets in Glasgow, and attracted many Irish immigrants, who came to Glasgow to escape the potato famine. The book *Glasghu Facies* writes of the strong Irish links of Bridgegate 'We have Lodging-Houses kept by the O'Doughertys, the Trainers, and Widow Carroll; there is the Londonderry Hotel for the Orangemen, and the Emerald Isle Tavern for the Papists; spirit cellars are kept by the Kellys, the Connaghans and the Macnamees'.

Opposite the Bridgegate junction with Saltmarket the shop marked 'Homelectrix' marks the spot of an old tenement known as Silvercraig's Land, which was owned by the Campbell family, who were merchants in the town. Oliver Cromwell stayed here on a visit to Glasgow, and attended a service by an early Barony minister called Zachary Boyd. Boyd's sermon was scathing about Cromwell, whose officers wanted to turn their pistols on the preacher, but Cromwell got his revenge by inviting Boyd to dinner and having him kneel for three hours of prayer. All the tenements on the left hand side of Bridgegate have disappeared with some modern housing now in its place.

The tenements at 3 to 21 St. Margaret's Place were completed in 1905 under the direction of the City Engineer, A. B. McDonald, as part of the City Improvement Trust initiative. The whole Saltmarket area had become dilapidated and run down by the middle of the 19th century, and the city authorities embarked on a programme to demolish the old closes and vennels, to be replaced with modern tenements of the day. Glasgow photographer Thomas Annan captured the district on film, showing the old buildings and obvious poverty which dominated.

In this March 1973 view of Merchant Lane looking north, on the left hand side is the back wall of the Fish Market. On the right are a number of small commercial premises including James Alexander, fish salesmen, who operated here for over 40 years. The lane takes its name from the Merchants Hall, which stood in the vicinity and was built in 1659, with a steeple being added six years later, which is the only remaining part of the structure.

At Nos. 64 to 76 Clyde Street stands the Fish Market, completed in 1873 and further extended in 1903. The architects were Clarke & Bell, who adorned their design with two pairs of double Tuscan columns, and sea horses. In 1977 the market closed and operations moved up to Blochairn. In the early 1980s the building was converted into a Covent Garden style trendy shopping venue known as the Briggait Shopping Centre, but it proved unsuccessful, with many believing it was in the wrong part of town to attract high end customers.

The Fish Market has some attractive sculpture at roof level, with a portrait of Queen Victoria flanked on each side by winged hippocampi (sea horses). The sculptor is unknown.

In the early 19th century the population of Glasgow increased rapidly. Many who came to the city were from the Highlands or Ireland, at Bridgegate the Irish established an enclave. An open air clothes market was established and in 1831 with over 1600 hawkers and dealers trading in the district, the area became known as 'Paddy's Market'. The market was relocated in 1869 when the railway viaduct leading into St. Enoch's was built, and the traders moved to Shipbank Lane. The sign on the wall offers 'Stalls to Let' within Paddy's Market, many of them inside the railway arches. Others would simply spread their wares on the ground. It was a favourite haunt of Glaswegians looking for a bargain, or to just observe life, and there was some controversy in May 2009 when it permanently closed.

This attractive four storey tenement still occupies the corner site at Stockwell Street and Bridgegate, and dates from 1905, to a design by A.B. McDonald. The photograph was taken in January 1977 and the tenants on the first floor have yet to remove Christmas decorations from their window. The building is of a superior design with aedicules adorning the second floor windows. These are openings on doors or windows that are framed with columns and a pediment, and although not unique on Glasgow tenements, they are not common.

Looking north along Stockwell Street in March 1973. The street was originally known as Fishergate and had a draw well on its east side. Throughout the old town wells were the principal source of water supply, and in 1801 there were around 30 supplying the needs of the citizens. In the 1850s the piping of water from Loch Katrine provided this vital resource to industrial Glasgow. The bridge, advertising Carlsberg lager, was removed in 1978 and carried the railway across the street to St. Enoch's Station.

The curved tenement at 96 Clyde Street is covered in scaffolding in January 1977 as the demolition teams remove anything that has resale value before knocking the building down. At the top of the four storey structure the inscription 'Victoria Building' can be seen on the pediment, the building taking its name from the Victoria Bridge, which crosses the Clyde at this point. The corner site is now occupied by a block of modern flats.

Shoppers enjoy the summer weather in Stockwell Street, probably unaware of the ancient history of the street. It dates from 1345 and formed the western boundary of the old town. The street became popular with the merchant class, including many holding public office as Baillies, and was also the location of horse and cattle markets. As Glasgow developed into a major industrial force, what had been the old town became depopulated, being replaced with commercial buildings and retail shop premises. Nothing remains of this view, being replaced with modern outlets, including the premises of Millers Art Shop, which can trace its roots back to 1834, retaining a tenuous link with the past. The building with the three dormer like windows at 28 Stockwell Street dated from the early part of the 19th century and was at one time the Garrick Temperance Hotel, a popular meeting place of the Abolitionist movement. To teetotallers it must have seemed like an oasis in a desert, as Stockwell Street boasted 18 public houses by 1875.

Argyle Street starts at the Trongate junction and runs through to Partick Bridge, although in recent years its route has been altered at Anderston due to modern developments and road systems. Standing sentry at the Stockwell Street corner is a former town-house dating from around 1763, with the ground floor being used as shops. Traffic is still travelling along this section of Argyle Street in 1973, which was later pedestrianised, which has encouraged shoppers and attracted buskers in more recent times. On the extreme right hand side the substantial Lewis's department store peers over the townscape.

The white coloured building at 182 to 184 Trongate was known as Spreull's Land. It belonged to an old Glasgow family of substance who had owned the ground from as early as 1712. In 1784 they built this tenement property, and it became one of Glasgow's most desirable addresses, complete with a hanging spiral stair internally, and described as *'a large and elegant tenement'*. By the early 1970s the ground floor was occupied by Virgo, a fashion store, and the Royal Bank of Scotland, separated by a pend, which led to the rear of the property. Nearby also stood Shawfield Mansion, the scene of a riot in 1725 when citizens attacked the building, which was the home of Daniel Campbell, Member of Parliament. He had supported the imposition of a tax on Scottish Malt, much to the anger of the local population.

Standing isolated at the corner of Trongate and Glassford Street is the former National Bank of Scotland, built in 1903 in a Baroque-Baronial style to a design by T. P. Marwick, and likened to The Scotsman Building in Edinburgh. The National Bank of Scotland was established in 1825 and merged ten years later with the Royal Bank of Scotland, but continued to trade as a separate entity until 1959. The dust on the east side of the bank signals the demolition of Spreull's Land in 1978.

The architecture in this image has not changed since July 1973 when the photograph was taken on Trongate looking east from King Street. The large building dominating the north side of Trongate was developed from 1904 onwards, and was built on the site of the Tontine Hotel. It was here also that Glasgow's first pavement was laid, and was known as the 'Plainstanes' used only by the Tobacco Lords and other town dignitaries. Morris's paint and wallpaper shop advertises Sunday opening, which was not a widespread practice at the time.

In the heart of what we now call the Merchant City, Candleriggs runs north from Trongate, and was laid out in 1668 in the heart of the old Glasgow town. Its name is derived from two separate sources, as a 'rigg' is an old term for a narrow strip of land, often at right angles to the thoroughfare. In 1658 the Town Council decided to move the risky manufacture of candles to the edge of town and Candleriggs was the location chosen, and this completes the derivation of its name. At the head of Candleriggs at Ingram Street, the Ramshorn Church dominates the view. It was completed in 1826 to a design by Thomas Rickman, and is built on the site of a former church dating from 1724.

Still occupying the corner site at Trongate and King Street, this ornate tenement was completed in 1900 as part of the development of the Glasgow Cross area, under a scheme by the city engineer, A. B. McDonald. The tenement has four upper floors and was designed in a mix of Flemish and Baronial architecture. On the ground floor City Cash Tailors are the incumbent, specialising in gents fashion wear. Despite the suggestion of their name, they readily accepted shopping cheques, issued by companies such as Provident and Caledonian, which allowed users to 'buy now, pay later'.

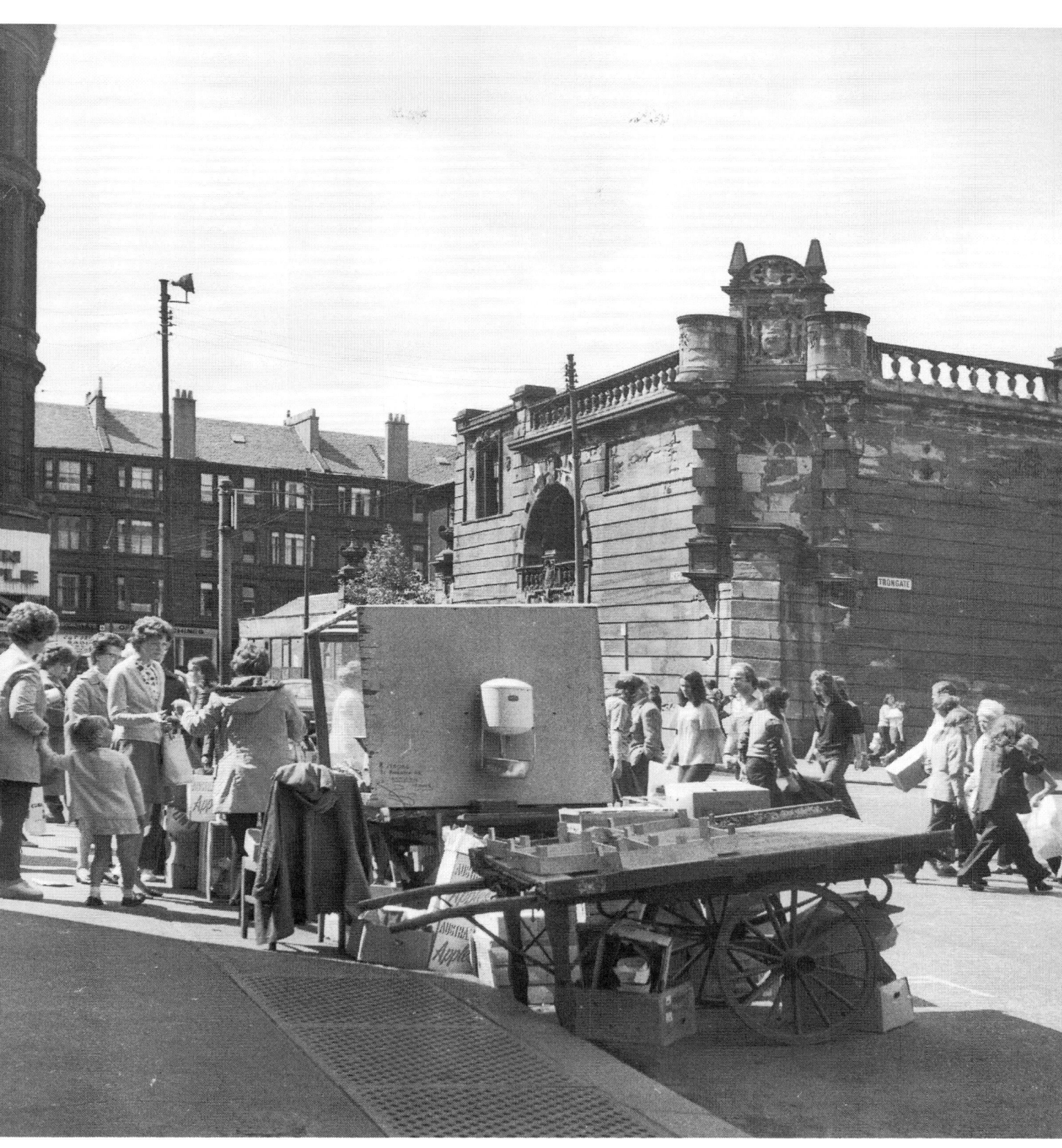

The street vendor offering fruit and vegetables from this barrow at the corner of Albion Street and Trongate appears to be doing brisk business in the warm July weather in 1973. To the left hand side, the premises of John Temple occupy the Trongate corner with Chisholm Street, and offer 'off the peg' and 'made to measure' suits to the male population of the city. Many men would pay their garments up on a weekly payment plan, ensuring they maintained their dapper appearance.

At Nos. 10 to 28 King Street is a commercial building built in 1902 to a design by James McKissack. It was a multi-occupancy premises, providing many small businesses with a workshop, store or office in the heart of the city. In the distance on Candleriggs, the large sign of department store Goldberg's attracts shoppers. Finding a parking space in July 1973 was easy.

Looking east along Parnie Street which runs parallel and to the south of Trongate. It was originally known as Gibson's Wynd, named after Provost Walter Gibson, before being renamed Princes Street. The tenements are a result of the City Improvement Trust Act of 1866 which enabled the city authorities to demolish the old wynds and vennels that characterised the area, followed by a programme of tenement building. The low rise structure with the crow stepped gable is the rear elevation of the Tron Kirk which dates from 1794, later being used as a joinery workshop.

This goods shed on the west side of King Street at Nos. 100 to 116 was built to serve the nearby (now demolished) St. Enoch's Station. It later became the bonded warehouse of William Teacher & Co. By the early 1970s it had fallen into disrepair, and the enterprising owner of the day was earning some revenue using it as a car park. Ironically, after it was demolished the site became an open air car park, still in use today.

This curved row of commercial premises, extending from 93 to 137 Howard Street was owned by the Glasgow and South West Railway company, who put this wedge of land on the side of St. Enoch's Station to good economic use. The taller building in the background was built as the offices of the railway company in 1905 to a design by H.E. Clifford, but best known today as the premises of gents' tailors and outfitters Slater & Co. The trendy Ford Capri completes the scene.

This tenement run at 1 to 39 Trongate still stands and is of a high quality. It took nine years to build and was completed in 1900 under the direction of City Engineer A. B. McDonald. It was designed in the French Renaissance style, three storeys high, with a pedimented dormer and comprises three and four apartment houses with inside bathrooms, at the time very desirable. Trongate is one of the original streets of Glasgow and was originally known as St. Thenew's Gate, named after the mother of St. Mungo. It became known as Trongait as it was here that the town had its tron, or weighing machine, where goods would be assessed for tax purposes.

The curved warehouse at 105 to 169 Bell Street was built in 1882 for Glasgow and South Western Railway Company. It was an early example of the use of cast iron columns supporting concrete arches as the frame of the building, with the rusticated curtain wall completing the structure. In the mid 1980s the warehouse was converted into flats as part of the regeneration of this part of what is now called the Merchant City. This portion of Bell Street was originally known as Graeme Street after Robert Graeme, a Sheriff-Substitute.

The Old College Bar on High Street is one of Glasgow's oldest hostelries, with its first licence granted in 1812, although parts of the building are claimed to date from 1510. The pub takes its name from the University of Glasgow that once stood opposite on High Street, before removing to Gilmorehill in 1870.

Nicholas Street takes its name from St. Nicholas Hospital which stood in the vicinity and was established in the 15th century by Bishop Andrew Muirhead, and was once known as Greyfriars Wynd. The one storey commercial building dated from 1893 and was the work of George Eadie, builder. It later became the premises of a fruit broker and then a wholesale stationer. Next door the scrap yard gate warns 'Beware of the Dog', an obvious bid to deter would be burglars. The stencilled chimney of the Bank of Scotland dominates the roof line.

The ornate building at 215 High Street at the corner with Nicholas Street was built in 1895 to a design by Salmon, Son & Gillespie for the British Linen Bank. The circular structure at roof level is known as a tempietto, and replicates a small temple. A plaque on the Nicholas Street elevation marks the birthplace of poet Thomas Campbell, who also has a statue in George Square. High Street is one of the most ancient of all thoroughfares in Glasgow, being the route from the Cathedral to the fishing village on the Clyde at Saltmarket.

Looking south down High Street in March 1973. On the left is High Street Goods Station. High Street was laid out at the beginning of the 12th century. It was the backbone of the old medieval town, with many primary routes leading off it, such as Rottenrow, Drygate and Gallowgate.

The white building at the corner of High Street and George Street has shops at street level and workrooms above. On George Street FW Holroyd were founded in 1912 and traded from the old spice market in Virginia Arcade selling floor coverings and furnishings, before specialising in picture framing and mouldings. Near to here stood the College Street Medical School, whose owner Granville Sharp Patterson was accused of receiving corpses from the Ramshorn Burial Ground in 1814. He was tried and acquitted at Edinburgh. In 1832 the Anatomy Act ensured medical students were henceforth able to study corpses provided by local poor houses and not grave robbers.

This long gone building at Shuttle Street, close to the College Street junction, was once St. Paul's Parish Mission Rooms, where religious meetings were held, as well as help and support to the local community dispensed. In the 1960s it became the premises of greengrocer chain Malcolm Campbell, convenient for the nearby fruit market at Candleriggs.

On the right hand side in July 1973, at No. 29 College Street stands the Bell Telephone Exchange, built around 1922 on the site of the Albion Halls, to cope with the increasing demand for telephones in the district. Next door at Nos. 19 to 23 is a commercial building, with eighteen windows per floor, spread over three storeys, allowing plenty of natural light into the working area. The building was used by various businesses, mainly in the garment manufacturing sector. The low-rise white painted building on High Street was for many years the premises of Alston's Tea Rooms.

The building fronting on to College Street with the double wall-head chimney was built on the site of the Barony Parochial Chambers and was used for many was years by A. Campbell & Co., fruit brokers. Next door at No. 6 a sign advertising McEwan's beer marks the Exchange Bar, which was also known as the Hi-Spot Bar. The distinct building with the columns rising from the first floor level, fronting on to High Street, was one of a pair standing sentry at the entrance to College Street. They were built in 1793 to a design by Robert Adam as accommodation for the professors of Glasgow University.

In June 1974 the north side of College Street awaits demolition. The pub on the ground floor of the bricked up tenement was the Exchange Bar, also known as the University Bar. At the time of its closure it was trading as The Croft Inn. Completing the scene, the dilapidated premises of shoe retailer High Walk occupies the corner site with High Street.

Occupying the corner site of College Street and Shuttle Street in April 1973 was the premises of Marshall & Steven Ltd., wholesale grocers. It was formerly a laboratory of the Chemistry Department of the University of Glasgow when it was located in High Street. The glass and glazed panelled building at right angles to College Street on Albion Street is the former Daily Express Building, built in 1936 for Lord Beaverbrook. It later became the premises of the *Glasgow Herald* and *Evening Times*.

Only the telephone exchange building on the extreme left remains of this view looking down Shuttle Street from March 1973. Marshall & Steven originally operated from Kingston Street, south of the river, and specialised as tea merchants and tinned fruit importers. The low rise building at the bottom of Shuttle Street has been replaced with a modern building housing an Italian restaurant, part of the trendy Merchant City. In the foreground the Linwood built Hillman Imp finds a place to park on a fenced in patch of waste ground.

The substantial commercial buildings at Nos. 5 to 13 Shuttle Street were typical of the area, housing many diverse businesses, with fruit broking the most prominent trade. In recent times the Shuttle Street area has been the subject of archaeological digs, searching for evidence of the Dominican Friary which once stood in the vicinity, and whose residents wore black habits and were known as Black Friars.

The buildings occupying the corner of Montrose Street and George Street have totally disappeared, to be replaced by a modern office block owned by Glasgow City Council. The tall building with the mansard roof was known as St. Mungo's Leather Works, the premises of W. Walker & Sons. A few doors down were more leather works dating from the early 1800s. At the end of the block is the former Sanitary Chambers building, on the Cochrane Street corner, dating from 1897, and now forming part of the City Chambers complex.

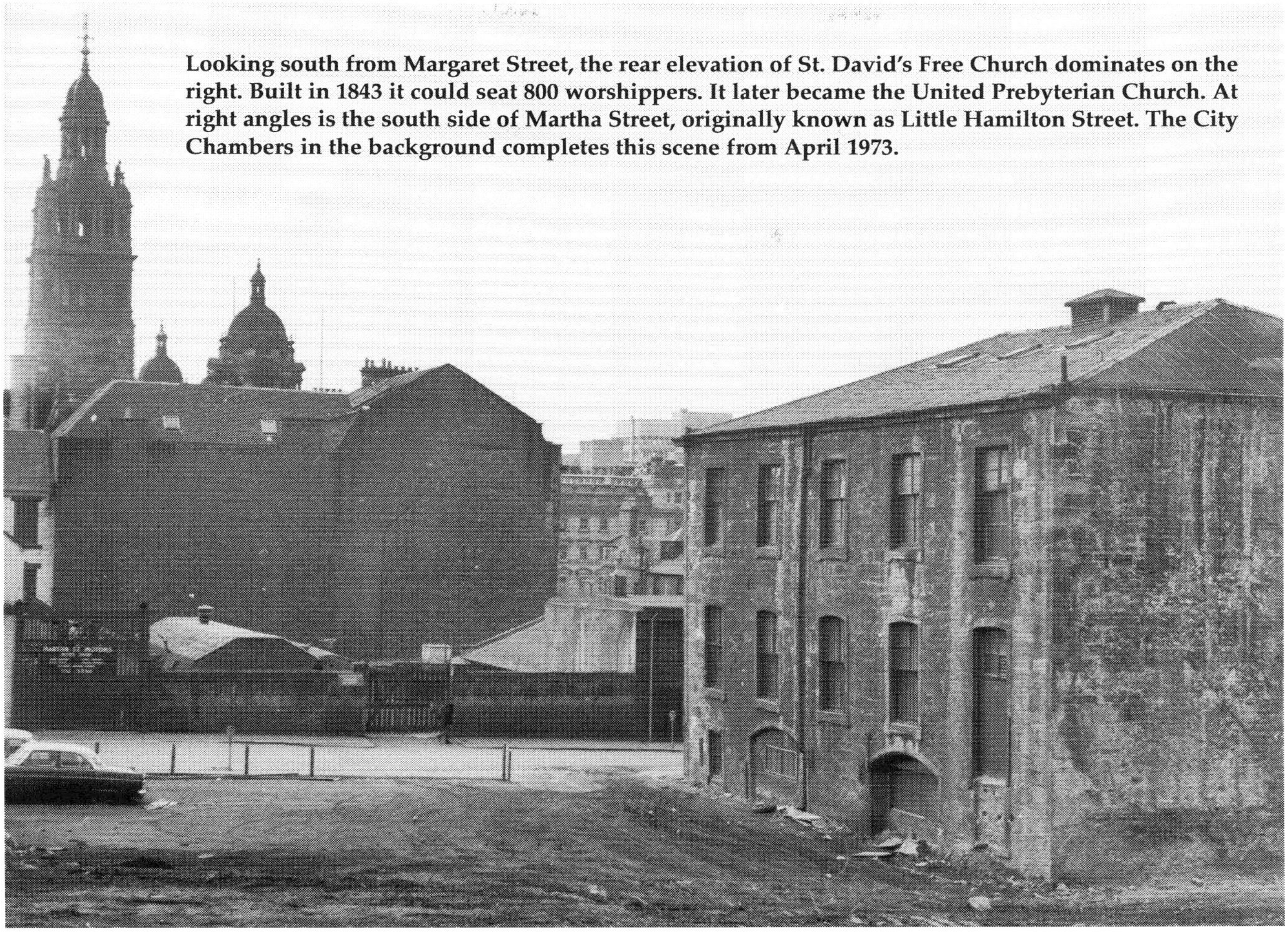

Looking south from Margaret Street, the rear elevation of St. David's Free Church dominates on the right. Built in 1843 it could seat 800 worshippers. It later became the United Prebyterian Church. At right angles is the south side of Martha Street, originally known as Little Hamilton Street. The City Chambers in the background completes this scene from April 1973.

North Frederick Street, looking south on to George Square, was opened in 1787 and named after Frederick, Duke of York, the second son of King George 3rd and Queen Charlotte. The George Bar is next to Frederick Lane. The pub was named after George Slater, whose father owned the premises from 1870 to 1885.

The autumn sunshine of November 1973 reflects well on 50 to 58 George Square, and gives us a glimpse of what was lost. In recent years builders have honed their skills in the art of refurbishment, with many fine examples throughout the city, and given the opportunity would have saved this impressive building.

For a few years between the demolition and the building of George House in 1979 the site formed an extension to the open space of George Square. By the time of this photograph in 1975 the new green space had been planted with saplings, forming a pleasant little park.

Cochrane Street, laid out in 1787 was originally known as Cotton Street, as it was here that many of the cotton traders conducted their business. It was later named after Andrew Cochrane, who had been Lord Provost in 1760. The south side of the street is dominated by commercial buildings reflecting its history. The building with the dormer windows and pend leading to the rear, was for over 100 years the premises of James Walton & Co., wholesale stationers and paper merchants. The splayed corner is occupied by the Queen's public house, which decanted here from North Frederick Street following demolition.

The plain terrace of commercial buildings running west from Montrose Street on Cochrane Street dated from the late 18th century, and after demolition was replaced by Wheatley House, completed in 1995 for Glasgow City Council. The John Street U.P. Church at the corner dates from 1860 and was designed by J.T. Rochead. The Merchant City began to establish itself in the mid 1980s and the church became a bar and offices in 1988.

Wilson Street runs from Candleriggs westwards to Virginia Street. The street was laid out in 1778 and named after George Wilson, who ran a charity school in the vicinity. At No. 21 stood the Hangman's Rest public house. The premises were first licensed in 1836. It was named following a visit to the hostelry by the hangman from Duke Street Prison, in the company of the curator of the nearby County Buildings. Following a fire in the 1980s the pub was demolished.

Only the curved corner of the Fruit Market would be recognisable today, looking east along Wilson Street. The site occupied by the (now demolished) four storey high warehouse building on the corner with Candleriggs, was used as an open air market during the highly successful 2014 Commonwealth Games held in Glasgow. A.G. Barr, manufacturers of 'Irn Bru' had a pop-up retail outlet here.

This scene of Ingram Street photographed in May 1974 has barely changed, with the Corinthian portico of the Court House building dominating. It occupies the whole block of Wilson, Hutcheson, Brunswick and Ingram Streets, and was built in three separate phases during 1841, 1871 and 1892. It is no longer a public building and now houses mixed commercial businesses as well as a restaurant. The building to the left built in the baronial style, dates from 1856 and was the former warehouse premises of Campbell, Stewart and Macdonald.

Another unchanged view, this time looking north on Albion Street. The squat fruit market building is on the site of the former Central Police Office, and has now become a complex of bars and restaurants, with the internal courtyard used as an occasional market. Just beyond, the white coloured City Halls is used as an entertainment venue for concerts. Cutting across at right angles at the end of the street is the Albion Buildings at 56 to 64 Ingram Street dating from around 1875 and one of the first buildings refurbished as part of the Merchant City rebirth.

The pedimented commercial building at 67 to 71 Brunswick Street is occupied by Robert Gordon & Co., who were wholesale boot factors. Their building dated from around 1790, and was one of many constructed in the city at the end of the 18th century to meet the demand for factories and commercial premises, as Glasgow enjoyed a successful period of trading, particularly with America. To the right stands the more modern building from 1936, to a design by Thomson Sandilands & Macleod. Brunswick Street was laid out in the late 18th century and was named in honour of the House of Hanover.

This portion of Ingram Street was previously known as Canon Street and was laid out around 1360, being the route to a seminary which was in the area. It was later realigned and called Back Cow Lone before finally being renamed Ingram Street in honour of Archibald Ingram, who served as Provost in 1782. He was the brother-in-law of John Glassford, the influential Tobacco Lord. Close to this spot was an old draw well, but it was not popular with the citizens as it was felt the water 'tasted of the flavour of dead men's bones', on account of its close proximity to the nearby burial ground.

Looking west along Ingram Street, the line of buildings on the south side between Albion Street and Candleriggs has entirely disappeared. This stretch dated from the early 19th century and played home to numerous fruit brokers, giving them ready access to the Fruit Market at Candleriggs, halfway along a pend can be seen, which led into St. David's Court. The site is now an open air car park, characterised by an ornate mural on the wall of the market building.

Looking west along Ingram Street, the view is dominated by the Gothic style tower of St. David (Ramshorn Kirk) opened in 1826 to a design by Thomas Rickman, and capable of holding over 1100 worshippers. Adjacent is a graveyard, dating from 1719, and the final resting place of Pierre Emile L'Angelier, a Jersey born clerk, who was the clandestine suitor of socialite, and architect's daughter Madeleine Smith. L'Angelier died of arsenic poisoning and Madeleine was charged with his murder. She was taken to trial in Edinburgh but the verdict was 'Not Proven'. She later emigrated to America and died in 1928 in her nineties, and always denied committing murder. Madeleine is buried at Mount Hope Cemetery, Hastings on Hudson in New York State.

Looking south on Candleriggs, its west side reflects the commercial nature of the district. The two plain fronted warehouses date from the early 1800s. Just beyond the pedestrian is a pend, now secured with an iron gate, which led into Graham's Court. Further along with the ornate pediment at Nos. 87 to 99, is a warehouse built in 1873 with additions following a fire in 1912. It was the premises of Simons & Co., fruit brokers.

It comes as no surprise that the Fruit Market at Candleriggs attracted traders into the vicinity. At Nos. 121 to 123 on the west side are Carruthers, fruit brokers, whilst on the opposite side is the warehouse of George Macleod Ltd. also involved in the fruit trade. Occupying the corner site with Ingram Street is the Royal Bank of Scotland, which date from the 1930s, and are now in use as a coffee shop. The Ramshorn Kirk completes the scene from April 1974.

Candleriggs was laid out in 1724, on what had been corn fields, from Trongate to what is now known as Ingram Street. A rigg is an old Scottish word for a strip of land and the street led to a candle works, which would have been an important factory, producing the main light source of the time. On the right is the Fruit Market and City Halls, laid out on the site of a bowling green and acquired by the town council in 1816, who built a Bazaar here a year later, which was the fore-runner of the later market.

As Glasgow began to rapidly expand westwards in the late 18th century, Provost Andrew Buchanan of Drumpelier laid out Virginia Street in 1753, with the street name acknowledging the city's trading history in the tobacco and cotton trades with the Americas. At the head of the street is the rear elevation of the Union Bank Building, complete with cupola. It was built in 1841 on the site of Andrew Buchanan's Virginia Mansion, and later became the court building Lanarkshire House. Virginia Street became a commercial centre in the city, with numerous warehouses and business premises, and in the foreground of the west side of the street, are the premises of Stevens & Co. warehousemen.

This house occupying the corner site of Virginia Street and Virginia Place dated from around 1800, and would in its day have been a high end property in the old town of Glasgow. By 1973 the first floor accommodation was the premises of Zirell's gent's tailors, a slice of Saville Row in the heart of the city, where the discerning gentleman could have his clothes 'made to measure' rather than shop in the chain stores offering only 'off the peg' options. In Virginia Place the signage of Carriers' Quarters can be clearly seen. If a business had a delivery of goods to make to an outlying area, they could be taken to a number of Carriers' Quarters offices throughout the city, where a network of small hauliers would be used to carry out the delivery. The whole scene was swept away by demolition two years after the photograph was taken in September 1973.

October 1973 and the premises of Birrell and 'suede centre' occupy the ground floor of Nos. 5 to 11 Argyle Street, an old Glasgow town house dating from the 1760s. Argyle Street is an ancient route, and was originally part of the road leading west to Dumbarton Castle. It later became known as St. Thenew's Gait, named after the mother of Glasgow's patron saint, St. Mungo. Later still, it became known as Westergate, and eventually became Argyle Street, after the funeral procession of the fourth Duke of Argyll passed along the route in November 1770. Birrell were one of many confectionery manufacturers in Glasgow, and were direct rivals to R.S. McColl. Both companies tended to have retail outlets close to cinemas, where there was a ready market for their sweets with movie patrons.

At Nos. 33 to 37 Argyle Street was another town house from the late 18th century serving as commercial and retail premises a couple of hundred years or so later. High street big names Easiephit and John Temple occupy the lucrative ground floor, whilst the upper floors were the Argyle Auction Rooms. The stencil on the front facade at first floor level directs clients to the long gone pawn-broking premises of A.J. and I.S. McLeod, who later traded in the Govan area. Their entrance is through the pend to the left at No. 31, which led into Moodie's Court, named after a family who owned ground in the vicinity.

To the right are the premises of ladies outfitters Graftons, occupying a modern building. It was here that on the afternoon of 4th May 1949, that a fire broke out. It spread very rapidly, resulting in the death of thirteen young female workers, aged between 15 and 23. Five others were led to safety in a precarious rescue, by two male co-workers along a five inch wide ledge at roof level to the safety of the adjoining Argyle Cinema. This tragedy is sadly only one of many such in Glasgow, giving it the 'Tinderbox City' reputation.

Running east from the St. Enoch Hotel, in May 1974, was North Drive, a narrow thoroughfare which ran through to Dunlop Street. The St. Enoch Shopping Centre now covers the entire scene.

The St. Enoch Hotel was one of the great railway hotels built during the boom years of the Victorian period in 1879 on the site of the Surgeons Hall, to a design by Thomas Wilson for the Glasgow and South West Railway. It contained over 200 bedrooms and was at one time the largest hotel in Scotland, and the third largest in Europe. During the Second World War the Royal Navy located its shore-based HMS *Spartiate* at the hotel. They were responsible for security and safety on the River Clyde, with the danger of enemy mines an ever present risk.

The distinct frontage of St. Enoch's Station was an iconic image in Glasgow for many years. The station was opened by the City of Glasgow Union Railway in 1876 to service the south west of Scotland. It was one of the four main railway stations in Glasgow, and had twelve platforms, covered by its distinct glass barrel roof. In 1923 a train over-shot the buffers and crashed with the loss of sixteen lives and 64 passengers injured. In 1966 the station was a victim of the rationalisation of the railway network. Only Queen Street and Glasgow Central remain of the 'big four', with Buchanan Street suffering the same fate as St. Enoch, which was demolished in 1977. The site is now covered by the St. Enoch Shopping Centre.

St. Enoch Square was laid out in 1782 and is named after St. Thenew. This 1973 view of the west side of the square remains unchanged. The slightly lower building at the far end of the terrace was the offices of William Teacher & Sons, scotch whisky distillers from 1875 until 1991. The company was known in its early days for its 'dram shops'. Wedged between the Square Peg public house and the Royal Bank of Scotland, a couple of shops find it necessary to roll out their awnings in the bright sunshine of May 1974.

The three storey buildings on the south side of Howard Street date from the early 19th century, and in 1974 were in mixed commercial use. The pub occupying the Dixon Street corner on the extreme right was known as The Lorne, later renamed 'Fat Boab's', perhaps a tribute to the pal of D. C. Thomson creation 'Oor Wullie'. Next door is the Adelphi Hotel which has also changed name, and is now the budget St. Enoch Hotel. The taller building on the extreme left is a printing works, built around 1868 for McCorquodale & Co, founded in 1846.

This covered passageway below St. Enoch Station at Nos. 51 to 71 Howard Street is reminiscent of an Italian 'piazza'. The New Zealand Lamb Shop was in the ownership of J & W Galloway, the well-known Glasgow butcher chain. The elderly man, resplendent with his 'bunnet' appears to be enjoying his stroll in the early spring sunshine of March 1975. The substantial stone columns bear the weight of St. Enoch Station above.

This former church building at 130 Howard Street was for many years the premises of Cockburn & Co., manufacturing chemists. It was built around 1870 as an E.U. Church, and had a short life as a house of worship, as it had become commercial premises by the 1890s.

The tall four storey tenement on the corner of Clyde Street and Stockwell Street was once known as the Victoria Buildings, with a commanding view over the river towards Gorbals. The busy scene from September 1973 is characterised by the styles of the day, with flair trousers and platform shoes clearly in vogue. To the rear of the warehouse carpet was the former Dreghorn mansion.

Viewed from Ropework Lane in May 1975 the rear elevation of the Dreghorn Mansion is still distinct. It was built in 1752 for Glasgow merchant Robert Dreghorn of Ruchill, known locally as 'Bob Dragon.' He was by all accounts an ugly man with a very poor complexion, who had very little luck with the fairer sex, which led him to commit suicide in 1806, with local folklore claiming the mansion house to be haunted.

This view of Argyle Street from Oswald Street towards Robertson Street is now the location of the upmarket Radisson Hotel. In July 1975 Grandfare occupied the majority of the retail space as the growth of supermarkets gathered pace. At No. 303 the distinct pawnbroker's sign of three brass balls marks the premises of Robert Biggar Ltd. who established their business in 1830 and trade to the present day.

The Clyde Navigation Trust offices at 16 Robertson Street were built in two phases. The original building was completed in 1886 and is characterised by the five arched bays at ground level, three Corinthian columns rising from the second floor level, and an ornate pediment at roof level. The rounded corner on to Broomielaw was added in 1908 with its distinct dome and sculpture. The much plainer warehouse at Nos. 22 to 24 was home to nut and bolt stockholder James Young & Co.

The three storey commercial building at Nos. 70 to 74 Broomielaw dates from 1840, as can be seen from the date-stone on the wall-head chimney. Just below is a plaque with a galleon, indicating the building's links to Glasgow's maritime past. The building has played host to a rope-maker as well as a ship's chandler's, and part was also used as Diamond's Temperance Hotel, which would have been ideally placed for merchant trade. The quirky rowing boat mounted on the wall at Nos. 66 to 68 marks the Waterfront public house, the site having been licensed since 1846, and also variously known as The Doune, The Double Six and latterly 'Frank's Place', before its demolition in 2005. Mackinlay's Scotch Whisky is advertised on the billboard above the pub. They were founded at Leith in 1847 and in 1907 were the official suppliers of scotch whisky to Ernest Shackleton's Antarctic expedition.

The ornate premises of Chelmis Limited are ideally placed to serve their ships chandler's business, at 118 to 120 Broomielaw by the side of the River Clyde. It occupied the site of the former Liverpool and Dumfries Hotel, which was one of a number of hotels and hostels on Broomielaw, providing accommodation for visitors to Glasgow's dock area.

The Alhambra Restaurant at 350 Argyle Street was in an ideal location to catch lunchtime diners as well as theatregoers to the nearby venue of the same name. In the adjacent West Campbell Street the City Rendezvous public house plied its trade, on a site licensed since 1854.

Argyle Street leads west towards the district of Anderston, which began as a weaving village. As industrialisation took hold, the weaver's cottages were replaced with power loom factories, with Manchester born Henry Houldsworth establishing a mill at Cheapside Street. Reports from the day indicate that he was not a model employer, and drove his workforce hard. By 1824 Anderston had become a burgh in its own right, but by 1846 it faced the inevitable fate of many districts, by being annexed into an ever-growing Glasgow and losing its identity. To the left the modern office block and Anderston Bus Station offer a contrast to the 19th century tenements.

The plain building at the corner of West Campbell Street and Holm Street dated from the 1840s and by the mid 1970s had become the premises of W. C. Martin & Co. electrical engineers. Next door the striking Clydesdale Bank Building, fronting on to Argyle Street is from a design by Baird & Thomson in 1892, with the bank operating from the ground floor, and business chambers above. The former bank is now the Picolo Mondo restaurant.

This curved commercial building on Bothwell Street was known as the Eagle Buildings and dated from 1854 to a design by Alexander Kirkland for the Chartered Building Trades Merchants. This portion of Bothwell Street was previously known as Bothwell Circus. In the background the Albany Hotel dominates the skyline. Completed in 1973 it was used by the St. Andrew's Sporting Club as a venue for professional boxing bouts. The 15 storey high hotel was demolished in 2007 to make way for a future development.

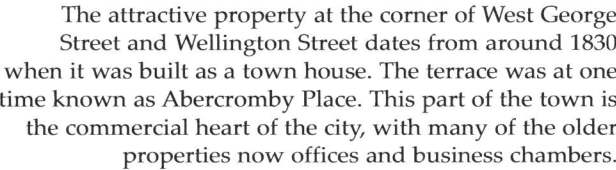

The attractive property at the corner of West George Street and Wellington Street dates from around 1830 when it was built as a town house. The terrace was at one time known as Abercromby Place. This part of the town is the commercial heart of the city, with many of the older properties now offices and business chambers.

At No. 278 West George Street stands St. Jude's Free Presbyterian Church, built in 1839 in a Greek style to a design by architect John Stephen. In recent times, many city centre churches have lost their congregations, and in 1975 St. Jude's was converted into an office suite. It now serves as a bar restaurant.

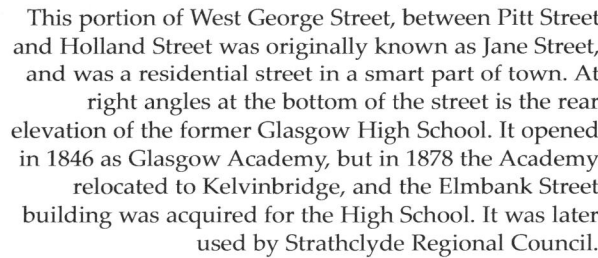

This portion of West George Street, between Pitt Street and Holland Street was originally known as Jane Street, and was a residential street in a smart part of town. At right angles at the bottom of the street is the rear elevation of the former Glasgow High School. It opened in 1846 as Glasgow Academy, but in 1878 the Academy relocated to Kelvinbridge, and the Elmbank Street building was acquired for the High School. It was later used by Strathclyde Regional Council.

Built in 1897 is the Freemasons Hall at 100 West Regent Street, to a design by J. L. Cowan. The building is adorned with a sun motif at roof level, and set in niches below are statues of St. John the Baptist on the left, and St. John the Evangelist to the right. The halls were used by the Provincial Grand Lodge of Glasgow as well as being used as business chambers.

*Facing page*: The impressive Grosvenor Building at 72 to 80 Gordon Street was built as a warehouse in 1859 to a design by Alexander Thomson. It was burnt down in 1864 and rebuilt within two years with the original facade being retained. In 1907 upper floors were added, and by this time it was the Grosvenor Restaurant, a top spot for Glasgow diners. Fate does not appear to have been on the side of the Grosvenor, as it was once again gutted by fire in 1967, and once more underwent a rebuilding programme.

Nestled at 17 to 21 Drury Street stands one of Glasgow's best known public houses the Horse Shoe Bar. There were licensed premises on the site from 1846, and in 1884 it was named The Horse Shoe by new owner John Scouller, reflecting his love of horses. It was later bought by its manager, a man called John Young Whyte, whose initials can be seen set into the stonework. There is an upstairs dining room which doubles up as a karaoke venue, and proves popular with Glasgow's pub going citizens. In 2007 the owners introduced a standard pub menu and decided to stop selling pies, which traditionally accompanied a pint of beer. There was outrage, and following an internet petition, where over 65,000 hits were recorded, the humble 'pie and a pint' was

Looking west along West George Street St. George's Tron Church occupies its island location at Buchanan Street and St. George's Place, later renamed Nelson Mandela Place. The church was built in 1807 to a design by William Stark, who was also responsible for the Lunatic Asylum building on Parliamentary Road, now demolished. The white building on the left was once the Victoria Hotel but the terraced row has been demolished, and replaced with modern offices. The no entry sign on the extreme left marks the spot of Anchor Lane, named after the Anchor Line, who had offices at nearby St. Vincent Place. It was previously known as St. Vincent Lane.

October 1973 and the Evangelical Union Church at 123 Dundas Street appears to await demolition. Built in 1856 to a design by John Burnet, it could accommodate 800 worshippers, and later became Dundas Street Congregational Church. The site is now occupied by Buchanan Galleries. The edge of Dundas Street Bus Station, opened in 1944, can be seen on the left.

Occupying the corner site of Dundas Street and Cunningham Street was the Free Tron Church, built around 1845 to a design by John Stephen. It was used for a time as church halls by St. George's Tron Church. In the background, to the left, the cooling towers of Port Dundas Power Station can be seen. Built in 1954 they were the largest of their kind in Europe at the time. Dundas Street was named after Sir Laurence Dundas who was pivotal in the construction of the Forth and Clyde Canal, completed in 1790, and still very much a part of the Glasgow landscape.

The white house at the corner of Bath Street and Hope Street dates from around 1805 and is an example of Glasgow's rapid growth towards the west in the early part of the 19th century. The Blythswood area soon became one of the most sought after addresses in the city. Around this time William Harley had established a business selling water throughout the city from hand carts; he went on to build the city's first public baths, which led to the present name of Bath Street. Heading south down the gradient is Hope Street, originally named Copenhagen Street but later changed to acknowledge Sir John Hope for his bravery during the Peninsular War.

The dignified, but derelict premises of glass and china wholesalers, Matthew McLaughlin & Sons were hijacked in their latter days by the tacky advertising of Lanyon-Cook Ltd. This stretch of Renfrew Street between Renfield Street and Hope Street was dominated through its history by the multi- occupation of commercial premises by companies involved in all manner of trades and professions.

The attractive St. John's Wesleyan Church which stood on the north east corner of the West Nile Street and Sauchiehall Street junction, was completed in 1883 to a design by McKissack and Rowan, and could seat 850 worshippers. Like many churches in the city it was demolished as part of the redevelopment of the area. The site is now occupied by modern shopping outlets.

At the corner of Maitland Street and McPhater Street stands Cowcaddens Free Church, completed in 1872 to a design by Campbell, Douglas and Sellars. It later became Cowcaddens U.F. Church and closed as a place of worship in the late 1960s. It is now the National Piping Centre, opened in 1996, with an auditorium capable of holding 180 people, as well as having twelve practice and tuition rooms. In the background, with the arched windows stands Orient House. Built in 1895 as a warehouse, it later became a lodging house for working men, and is now an apartment block.

Like the Gorbals and Townhead, Cowcaddens suffered wholesale demolition during the 1960s and 70s, leaving the district barely recognisable. This tenement at the corner of Cowcaddens Street and Airdrie Street is awaiting its inevitable demolition. Still hanging on in 1975 was the Kiwi Bar, the site of licensed premises since the 1850s. It was originally known as the Barnsmore, but was renamed as the Kiwi Bar in the early 1960s by two owners who served in the navy together, visiting New Zealand on their travels. The pub closed the year after this photograph was taken.

The tenements at Nos. 6 to 42 Cowcaddens Street await demolition as they reach the end of their useful life in 1975. In the background the multi-level car park and the College of Building and Printing are all that now remains of the scene. Much of the district disappeared from the 1970s onwards as the city was redeveloped and the 'Coocaddens' that Francie and Josie loved was lost forever.

Cowcaddens Street was at one time one of the principal shopping districts in central Glasgow, and ran from 179 West Nile Street to the New City Road and Garscube Road junction. It was a busy thoroughfare and boasted Milton House, the premises of Dallas's department store as well as a number of entertainment venues including the Prince of Wales Theatre and the Bijou Picture and Variety Palace. The street was named after the lands of Cowcaddens which were used by herdsmen to graze their cattle on the edge of the old town, which they would approach via Cow Loan, which followed the line of the present day Queen Street.

The tenements at 25 to 37 Cowcaddens Street 'cheek by jowl' with the sharp, angular commercial building at 152 to 172 Renfield Street, cordoned off at street level with corrugated sheeting.

The ornate warehouse building at the west corner of Gallowgate and Watson Street dates from the early 1870s and is believed to be from a design by architect James Hamilton. The Chrystal Bell public house was originally known as Rutherford's, and boasted a dining room as well as a public bar. It was later owned by the partnership of Chrystal and Bell, with the Chrystal family having a background in the spirit and distilling trade, whilst the Ayrshire born Bell family had a butchery business before becoming involved in the shipping trade. The low rise, white building nearest to Glasgow Cross was for many years the drapery department of the Co-operative, and later D & F Woodhouse's, home furnishers.

A busy Glasgow Cross looking south down Saltmarket seems awash with alcohol adverts, with Haig Whisky and Norseman Lager choosing the high vantage of the tenement gable, whilst the now gone Glasgow Cross Railway Station building sports a Crawford's Whisky poster. Saltmarket leads down to the River Clyde. It was previously known as Waulkergate, where waulkers or cloth workers once lived. It was renamed Saltmarket after becoming a place where salt used to preserve food, in the days before refrigeration, was sold. Glasgow was an important centre in the exporting of barrels of salted fish to France and Holland.

These tenements in Saltmarket were built in the 1890s, replacing the old closes and vennels which dominated the Glasgow Cross area. The shops on the ground floor provided good rental income for the property owners. The gable of No. 122 Saltmarket provides an ideal backdrop for billboards advertising alcohol and cigarettes.

St. Andrew's Parish Church takes centrepiece in St. Andrew's Square. Its design by Allan Dreghorn is based on St. Martins-in-the-Field in London, and took sixteen years to complete in 1756. The stonework was by master mason Mungo Naismith, whilst the internal plasterwork was the work of Thomas Clayton. When the church was opened the Molendinar Burn ran close by, on its way to converge with the River Clyde. In recent years the church has been used as a venue for concerts and music.

Occupying the corner site of Greenhead Street and Turnbull Street is St. Andrew's by the Green Church. It was completed in 1752 and is the oldest surviving Episcopalian church in Scotland. The masons responsible were William Paull and Andrew Hunter. It was known as the 'English' church because Episcopalians were Scottish Anglicans but also referred to as the 'Whistlin' Kirk' on account of having an organ installed to provide music during its services, contrary to the practices of other branches of Christianity at the time. In 1988 the church was converted into offices. To the right the gable of the Hide and Tallow Market of 1890 is visible.

Typical Glasgow weather in March 1973 hangs over the Saltmarket area. In the background the Merchant's Steeple on Bridgegate rises above the scene, whilst the white painted warehouse premises of Gratispool adds some light. The company were photographic processors, and many a camera spool was sent here to be perhaps turned into treasured images. Shops at street level prop up the tenement on the corner of Saltmarket and Jocelyn Square.

Looking west from Steel Street, the two tenements standing, sentry-like, either side of Saltmarket at Bridgegate dominate the scene. On the left the Old Shipbank tenement, which was remodelled in 1904 by R. Horn, stands on the site Glasgow's Ship Bank, founded in 1750 to support the city's growing trade with the Americas. In 1836 it merged with the Glasgow Bank, eventually coming under the umbrella of the Bank of Scotland. The ground floor is made up by the Old Ship Bank public house, a popular karaoke haunt for its patrons. To the right is one of the collection of tenements in Saltmarket which replaced the old closes and vennels, prevalent in the area, which disappeared under the City Improvement Trust initiative, with the tenement dating from 1893.

The tenement with the ornate dome at the corner of Greendyke Street and Saltmarket marks the location of Mumford's Penny Geggie, which was an early form of music hall, established in 1843 by Bedford born William Mumford. This form of entertainment became very popular in the second half of the 19th century, with the Panopticon on nearby Trongate a surviving example of this type of establishment. Mumford's entertained until the 1870s when it closed. Afterwards it became a clothes market, which was eventually demolished and replaced with the tenement seen. The pub just visible on the right hand side is the Whistlin' Kirk, taking its name from the nearby St. Andrew's by the Green Church.

On the left hand side of this April 1973 view of Saltmarket is the edge of the High Court of Justiciary building, completed in 1814 to a design by William Stark. It has been the venue for many infamous murder trials over the years, and arguably the most notorious was that of Peter Manuel in 1958 who received the death penalty. The last public hanging in the city was that of Edward William Pritchard, executed in front of a large crowd, outside the court buildings in 1865. The low rise building next to the court is the City Mortuary, built in the 1930s on the site of the former Dog and Bird Market, whilst on the right is the entrance to Glasgow Green.

This view of Saltmarket has changed little in the past 150 years, with the Tolbooth Steeple, railway bridge and City Improvement Trust tenements all still to the fore. Other parts of the Saltmarket district have changed beyond recognition, but the main thoroughfare running south from Glasgow Cross to the River Clyde remains a constant touchstone in the city's history.

This everyday scene from March 1973 shows people and traffic on Saltmarket going about their business. Occupying the corner of Saltmarket and St. Andrew's Street are the photographic premises of Charles Frank, established by the Lithuanian immigrant around 1907. He supplied the armed forces with navigation instruments and binoculars during the Second World War. The business closed in 1974 although former employees continued to use the trading name in their own venture in Edinburgh.

Running off the east side of Saltmarket is Steel Street and on its left hand side stands the Tent Hall, built for the United Evangelical Association on the site of a former timber yard, and dated from 1876. Prior to this the Association met in a tent on Glasgow Green. When the Steel Street hall was opened it attracted youngsters from surrounding districts, attracted by the lure of a cup of tea and a bun, which was earned by joining in with hymns and prayers. In 1977 it was still trying to attract worshippers with its 'Jesus Saves' sign, prominent on the front elevation. It has since been converted into housing.

Only the Scotia Bar on the right hand side, remains of this November 1973 view of the south west portion of Stockwell Street. There have been licensed premises on this site since 1815 when Robert Robertson began selling ales and spirits. Next door is the remains of the Metropole Theatre, built in 1875 as the Scotia Variety Theatre, on the site of what had been the Scotia Hall. It became known as The Metropole in 1897, and was a popular venue for Glasgow theatregoers. It was destroyed by fire in October 1961. The site is now occupied by a hotel.

This view of Trongate looking east from King Street affords a diverse selection of old Glasgow architecture. From left to right, the white painted offices and shops at the west corner of Albion Street is the work of architect J. T. Rochead from 1854. In recent times a public house here traded under the name of Rochead's. Next is the imposing five storey office building, built between 1912 and 1922 on the site of the former Tontine Hotel, which dated from 1874. Adjacent is the Tolbooth Steeple, completed in the 1620s, whilst nearest the camera is Tron Steeple, the tower dating from the 1590s with the steeple added around 30 years later. The arch at pavement level was cut through to improve pedestrian access in 1855.

The Tron Steeple marks the spot of the Laigh Kirk, or Low Kirk built in 1794 to a design by Robert and James Adam. The site had been the location of previous churches dating from 1484 and 1592. The elaborate wall to the left of the steeple dates from 1900 designed by the eminent architect J. J. Burnet, and screens off an air shaft servicing the Argyle rail line, which runs below. The wall has been refurbished and now carries a plaque commemorating the City of Glasgow Police.

The bright sun of July 1973 has prompted the shopkeepers on High Street to open out their awnings, to protect their window displays from discolouration. On the Bell Street corner is the shop of Peter Fisher, a business established in 1816, providing varnish, decorating sundries and house furnishings.

This dwelling at 16 to 18 Blackfriars Street was built in 1792 to a design by James Adam. It formed part of a development by John Stirling, whom the street was previously named after (Stirling Street). It had been the premises of Joseph Coyle, fruit merchants. In 1986 the premises were given a complete makeover, and became the hotel and restaurant Babbity Bowsters, quaintly named after a type of kilted Scottish dance.

This view looking south down High Street in April 1973 seems eerily quiet, with not a car in sight and a lone pedestrian. The University of Glasgow was founded in 1451 and at first held classes in the crypt of the Cathedral. In the 1660s the University built a new facility on the east side of High Street on what became the College Goods Station. The wall on the left, running down towards Bell Street, is the site of the old University. In the middle of the 19th century this part of Glasgow had become very run down. The University sold the land to the railways who wanted to establish a city terminus, and a new University was built at Gilmorehill, where it remains to this day.

The two impressive buildings flanking the College Street junction of High Street are identical and were known as the Professor's Lodgings. By the time this photograph was taken, they were already in a state of disrepair and foliage can be seen growing from the roof area. Demolition followed soon after, robbing the city of an architectural gem.